All about...

J.K. Rowling

Shaun McCarthy

www.heinemann.co.uk/library

Visit our website to find out more information about **Heinemann Library** books.

To order:

 Phone 44 (0) 1865 888066

 Send a fax to 44 (0) 1865 314091

 Visit the Heinemann Bookshop at www.heinemann.co.uk/library to browse our catalogue and order online.

First published in Great Britain by Heinemann Library, Halley Court, Jordan Hill, Oxford OX2 8EJ, part of Harcourt Education. Heinemann is a registered trademark of Harcourt Education Ltd.

© Harcourt Education Ltd 2003

Editorial: Lucy Thunder and Helen Cannons
Design: David Poole and Geoff Ward
Picture Research: Rebecca Sodergren and Kay Altwegg
Production: Edward Moore

Originated by Ambassador Litho Ltd
Printed and bound in Hong Kong, China by South China Printing

ISBN 0 431 17980 8
07 06 05 04 03
10 9 8 7 6 5 4 3 2 1

British Library Cataloguing in Publication Data
McCarthy, Shaun
Rowling, J.K. – (All About...)
823.9'14
A full catalogue record for this book is available from the British Library.

Acknowledgements
The Publishers would like to thank the following for permission to reproduce photographs: Aerospace Imaging p**7**; Associated Press p**20**; Laurence Cendrowicz/Katz Pictures p**4**; John Cleare pp**8**, **9**, **10**, **12**; Corbis pp**19** (Kim Sayer), **25** (Mark Peterson); Corbis/Sigman (Murdo Macleod) p**26**; Express Images p**17**; Ford Motor Company Ltd p**11**; Robert Harding pp**13**, **16**; Mirror Group p**18**; PA Photos pp**6**, **23**, **27**, **28**; Photofusion (Sally Lancaster) p**14**.

Cover photograph of J.K. Rowling at the *Harry Potter and the Goblet of Fire* book signing at Harrods in 2000, reproduced with permission of Camera Press (Richard Stonehouse).

Sources
The author and Publishers gratefully acknowledge the publications which were used for research and as written sources for this book.

An Interview with J.K. Rowling, Lindsey Fraser (Mammoth, 2000) pp**9**, **13**, **15**
In her own words, J.K. Rowling talks all about Quidditch, Beasts and Comic Relief – www.scholastic.com/harrypotter/author
J.K. Rowling, A Biography, Sean Smith (Michael O'Mara, 2001) p**11**
Meet J.K. Rowling – www.scholastic.com/harrypotter/author pp**24**, **25**

Fiction works by J.K. Rowling are cited in the text.

The Publishers would like to thank Stephen Noon for his assistance in the preparation of this book.

Contents

Any words shown in the text in bold, **like this**, are explained in the Glossary.

Who is J.K. Rowling?

Joanne Rowling is one of the most successful writers of books for young people ever. Her stories about Harry Potter, the 'ordinary boy' who discovers he is a wizard, are read by millions of children and adults all over the world. Her first book, *Harry Potter and the Philosopher's Stone*, was a huge success, almost from the day it came out. She has now sold over 195 million books worldwide!

▲ Joanne Rowling is probably the most popular and successful writer of books for children ever. Millions of adults also enjoy reading her books.

From struggle to success

Joanne always wanted to be a writer. She wrote her first 'book', about a rabbit, when she was six.

Like her hero Harry, she had struggles in her life before becoming famous. There were times when she had little money and she wrote *Harry Potter and the Philosopher's Stone* in cafés in her spare time. However, as Joanne says, 'When you dream, you can do what you like.'

Factfile

★ Date of birth	31 July 1965
★ Star sign	Leo
★ Eye colour	Blue
★ Hair colour	Blonde
★ Pets	'A very violent rabbit'
★ Hobbies	Travel, going to the theatre
★ Favourite food	Wizard candy (the chocolate frogs)
★ Favourite book	*Black Beauty* by Anna Sewell
★ Favourite wish	To be able to use the jelly legs curse
★ Personal motto	'Drago Dormiens Nunquam Titillandus' (the Hogwarts' **Latin** motto, which means 'Never tickle a sleeping dragon')

K is for...

Some **publishers** say that boys will not read books written by women. So Joanne's **agent** said she should disguise herself by using only her initial on her first book. But 'J' on its own was a bit short and Joanne does not have a middle name. So Joanne suggested adding a 'K' as a second initial, after Kathleen, her favourite grandmother. Joanne became known as J.K. and now millions of boys have read her books!

The Rowling family

When Peter Rowling, Joanne's father, was just eighteen he set out on a nine-hour train ride from London to Scotland. It was an old-fashioned train with carriages that had separate compartments, like little rooms. The seat next to him was taken by a stranger, Anne Volent, who was also eighteen. They were both in the navy, going north to their **postings**. By the time they reached Scotland they were firm friends.

Changing trains

Writers sometimes change things that happen in real life and use them in their stories. The train where Joanne's parents met was a steam train like the Hogwarts Express. It was going to Scotland. Hogwarts does not exist in the normal 'muggle' world, but Joanne has said she imagines it as being somewhere in the Highlands of Scotland.

◀ Joanne and her father, Peter.

Joanne is born

Just over a year later, Peter and Anne were married in London, where they both lived. They had decided that navy life was not for them. They moved from London to Yate, in Gloucestershire. Joanne, their first child, was born on 31 July 1965. Yate was a small modern town surrounded by fields. The Rowlings were keen for their children to grow up near to the countryside. Peter went to work making aeroplane engines for fighter planes in a factory in the nearby city of Bristol. Two years later, in 1967, Joanne's sister Dianne was born.

▲ The aeroplane factory in Bristol shown around the time when Joanne's father worked there.

Books and stories

There were always lots of books and bedtime stories in the Rowling house. Joanne remembers her father reading *Wind in the Willows* to her when she was ill with the measles. Joanne says she was mad about horses as a child and loved books, like *Black Beauty* by Anna Sewell and *The Little White Horse* by Elizabeth Goudge.

Off to school

When Joanne was three the Rowlings moved to a modern house in Nicholls Lane in the village of Winterbourne, close to Yate. A boy one year younger than Joanne lived a few doors away. He was called Ian Potter! Joanne organized games for them to play about wizards and witches, where she made up potions and magic spells.

Winterbourne, near Bristol, where Joanne lived from the ages of three to nine.

Starting school

Joanne's first school was St Michael's, Winterbourne's village school. Although she was rather quiet and shy, Joanne loved school. She remembers being taken to see ducks on the village pond, and a school trip to see the ships in Bristol harbour.

When Joanne was nine, her family decided to move further out into the country. They bought Church Cottage in Tutshill, a village in the beautiful Wye Valley on the border between England and Wales.

Joanne had a special reason for liking her home in Tutshill:

'Our cottage was next to the church. All our friends thought it was spooky living next to a graveyard, but we liked it. I still love graveyards...'

A sorting test

Joanne's new school in Tutshill had strict teachers – especially Mrs Morgan, who everyone was scared of. Mrs Morgan set a test to sort her new class into 'able' and 'less able' children. Joanne did not understand the test and scored only half a mark! She was put with other children who had not done well on the right-hand side of the room. Those who had done well sat on the left. Joanne says she remembered this when she invented the 'sorting hat' at Hogwarts. Mrs Morgan soon saw that Joanne was a bright girl, and moved her to the 'clever' side of the room.

▲ This beautiful countryside is near Joanne's childhood home in the village of Tutshill, in the Wye Valley.

Tutshill memories

Tutshill School was a gloomy, old-fashioned place, like some parts of Hogwarts. In her book, *Quidditch Through the Ages* (by Kennilworthy Whisp, a **pen name** that Joanne made up), one of the teams is the Tutshill Tornadoes!

Wyedean school

When Jo (as she now liked to be called) was eleven she went up to Wyedean School. This was a big, modern **comprehensive** in nearby Chepstow. Chepstow is a historic country town with a river and a castle. Wyedean was a shock for Joanne after the little village schools she had been to. She was still rather shy and quiet, but she became popular with pupils and teachers. Joanne liked school, especially English lessons, and enjoyed reading – at home and at school. She dreamed of becoming a writer.

▲ Wyedean Comprehensive, where Joanne was a pupil for seven years.

A fight

Joanne generally got on quietly with her work but sometimes serious students were picked on. Eventually Joanne got into a fight with another girl at school. Other students were impressed that Joanne, only 5 feet and 4 inches tall, fought back against a bigger girl. Joanne says, 'For a few days I was quite famous because she hadn't managed to flatten me. The truth was, my locker was behind me and it held me up.'

A blue Ford Anglia

When she was in the sixth form at Wyedean, Joanne met a new pupil called Sean Harris. They became great friends. Sean had a blue Ford Anglia car.

▲ Joanne's friend Sean had a Ford Anglia like this. One like it appears in *Harry Potter and the Chamber of Secrets*!

The real Snape

Joanne partly based Snape, Hogwarts' potions master, on John Nettleship, her chemistry teacher at Wyedean School. John Nettleship says Joanne may remember him as strict because she could not answer his questions – just like Harry in *Harry Potter and the Philosopher's Stone*:

'"Potter," said Snape suddenly. "What would I get if I added powered root of asphodel to an infusion of wormwood?" "I don't know," said Harry. Snape's lips curled into a sneer...'

Leaving home

Joanne did A Levels at Wyedean School, then went straight off to Exeter University in Devon. She was eighteen and keen to get away from small town life, where there was not much for young people to do. Joanne enjoyed films and there was not even a cinema in Chepstow.

New friends

At first Joanne found it hard to adjust to life away from home. However, she soon made new friends among the other students and enjoyed going to the theatre and cinemas in Exeter. Joanne studied French, and for part of her course spent a year teaching English in Paris.

In Paris Joanne shared a flat with a young Italian man and two young women – one Spanish, the other Russian. Quite a change from life in the sleepy Wye Valley! She loved her time there and spent a lot of time reading in her room when she was not teaching.

Part of Exeter University, where Joanne spent three years studying.

▲ Paris is full of interesting things to see and do and Joanne made the most of her time there.

Family illness

When Joanne was twelve her mother found out that she had multiple sclerosis, a disease that affects the nerve endings and gets worse with time. She had gradually become weaker and weaker, and now walked with sticks. Her mother's growing illness was a terrible sadness and worry for Joanne, who was far away from home.

Joanne says she enjoyed her time at university but she thinks that studying English would have fitted in better with her long-term dream of being a writer.

What Joanne says

Joanne has this to say about her decision to study French:

'It was a bit of a mistake. I certainly didn't do everything my parents told me, but I think I was influenced [affected] by their belief that languages would be better for finding a job ... So learn from my mistake – do what you want, not what your parents want!'

This was all she really wanted to do although she did not tell anyone about this secret.

Graduation

One of the things Joanne had to do to get her degree was to write a 3000 word essay, in French. She also ran up a £50 fine for overdue books from the university library! Joanne passed her **degree** and **graduated** from Exeter University in 1987. Her parents came to the special ceremony where the students who have passed their university courses receive their degrees. Joanne's mother was now in a wheelchair.

Off to London

On leaving university, Joanne moved to London and trained to be a secretary. She says this was another mistake. 'Me as a secretary? I'd be your worse nightmare!' Joanne tried different jobs, but could not find one she liked. For a while she worked for Amnesty International, a charity that helps imprisoned or **persecuted** people all over the world. She shared a flat in London with other girls.

▲ Joanne lived in Clapham (shown here) during part of the time she lived in London.

A secret writer

Joanne still planned to write for a living and spent her spare time writing as much as she could. At lunch times and in the evenings she would dash off on her own to a café to write. She began two books for adults during this time, but never finished them.

The great idea!

Joanne's boyfriend had moved to Manchester in 1990 and she was getting ready to join him. Then, sitting on a train after a weekend flat-hunting in Manchester, she suddenly had the idea for Harry Potter. Characters were pouring into her imagination – Ron, Hagrid, Peeves and Nearly Headless Nick. Joanne did not have a pen, so she had to remember everything. She says that this was a good thing. If she could not remember the ideas at the end of the journey they might not have been very good after all!

What Joanne says

On having her great idea, Joanne says:

'I have never felt such a huge rush of excitement. I knew that this was going to be such fun to write. I didn't know then that it was going to be a book for children – I just knew I had this boy, Harry.'

As soon as she got home, Joanne wrote down everything she could remember in a small notebook. This was the start of the first ever Harry Potter story. Her notes about Harry and Hogwarts quickly grew and filled up an empty shoebox that she used as a file. However it would be seven long years before *Harry Potter and the Philosopher's Stone* would be **published** as a book.

A death and a birth

Joanne began writing the opening chapters of *Harry Potter and Philosopher's Stone*. The story was soon going well, but life was not so good. She had moved to Manchester, and things between her and her boyfriend were not working out. Then her mother died. Joanne remembers being very unhappy: 'Then our flat in Manchester was burgled, and everything my mother had left me was stolen … I decided that I wanted to get away.'

Going abroad

In the early 1990s Joanne took a job teaching English in the city of Porto in Portugal. There she met Jorge Arantes, a journalist (someone who writes for newspapers). They fell in love and soon got married. The following year they had a daughter, called Jessica. Joanne was almost 28. She had a baby, three chapters of her first Harry Potter book written and the rest of the story planned. She remembers this time as 'the best time of my life'.

▲ Porto in Portugal, where Joanne went to teach English to Portuguese students.

Heading for Scotland

Unfortunately, things soon started to go wrong again. Her marriage to Jorge was unhappy. Her teaching job was due to end in the summer, and she was worried about how to earn money. In 1993, she decided to spend Christmas with her sister, who had moved to Edinburgh in Scotland. It was a very important visit. Joanne felt that Edinburgh was a place where she would be happy living, so she decided to stay there. This would mean leaving Jorge behind in Portugal. She had no money and no job. What would happen to the book she was still so far from finishing?

Joanne and Jorge get married,
16 October 1992.

Trust yourself

Joanne trusted that moving to Edinburgh would work out. In *Harry Potter and the Philosopher's Stone*, Harry has to trust that by following seemingly crazy instructions he will break through from the 'muggle' station to Platform 9 ^{3}/4, where the Hogwarts Express is waiting to take him to his new life:

'*Harry walked more quickly. He was going to smash right into that ticket box and then he'd be in trouble – leaning forward on his trolley he broke into a heavy run – the barrier was coming nearer and nearer – he wouldn't be able to stop – he closed his eyes ready for the crash...*'

The big break

Joanne had a difficult time when she arrived in Edinburgh. She was surviving on a small amount of **social security** money. She was living in a miserable flat full of mice. To make matters worse, Joanne and Jorge decided to get **divorced**.

Making plans

Joanne decided to train to be a teacher, which meant another year at college. She knew that this would take up most of her time, but she was desperate to finish her book.

The café and restaurant where Joanne sat and wrote most of her first Harry Potter book.

Time to write

Joanne wrote whenever she could. She would wheel Jessica round in her buggy. When Jessica fell asleep, Joanne would rush to Nicolson's café and write for a couple of hours. She only ever bought one coffee, but the staff let her sit in the corner and write. At weekends, she would go into the computer room at the college where she was training and type up what she had written.

Success!

Finally, after hours of writing whenever she could, and seven years after she first had the idea for Harry Potter, Joanne finished her book. She sent it to an **agent**, Christopher Little, in London. The agency liked the book and agreed to help Joanne find a **publisher**. They sent the book out to a dozen publishers, all of whom said they were not interested. Then, after nearly a year, the publishers Bloomsbury read it, liked it and said they would **publish** it. On 26 June 1997, *Harry Potter and the Philosopher's Stone* came out.

Book dollars

At first nothing much happened. Joanne started working as a part-time teacher. Then an American company said they wanted to publish her book in the USA. They were offering $100,000: about £65,000! It was more money than Joanne had ever imagined.

▲ Bloomsbury's offices are in Soho Square (shown here) in the middle of London – a very long way from Edinburgh, where Joanne wrote the book.

J.K. and Harry are stars!

Joanne's first Harry Potter book started selling well in the USA. In Britain people thought it was very good, too, and it won a book prize – the 1997 Smarties Gold Award. Encouraged by her success, Joanne decided not to be a teacher, but to try living as a writer. She began her second book. She knew that eager readers were waiting for it. It had to be at least as good as the first one! Now she could afford to move to a much nicer flat. She bought a computer so she could type up the new book at home.

She still spent some time writing in the café, making notes about characters and events that would go into the story. Although Joanne was becoming a famous author she was still a single mother and had to fit her writing around looking after young Jessica.

▲ Joanne signs a Harry Potter book for a young fan in New York in 2000.

Harry's schooldays

Joanne plans seven Harry Potter books, one for each of Harry's seven years at Hogwarts. In 2001 Joanne reported that she had already written the last chapter of the last Harry Potter book. She said she knows what will happen to all of the characters and admitted that not everyone will stay alive.

Just one year and one month after her first book appeared, her second, *Harry Potter and the Chamber of Secrets*, was **published**. It went straight to the top of the best-seller lists.

Hard work

As a successful author, Joanne began touring bookshops signing copies of her books. Hundreds of people were turning up to see her, and not all of them were children. There were **articles** about her in the papers. She was a writing star!

Most days Joanne was at her desk, working on the third book, *Harry Potter and the Prisoner of Azkaban*. This book came out just two years after *Harry Potter and the Philosopher's Stone* had appeared so quietly. It was released to bookshops after school time on the first day so children would not skip school to go and buy it! This third book was an instant best-seller.

A quiet private life

Joanne was a superstar, but she liked to live quietly at home. She hired an American nanny to look after Jessica to give herself more time to write. When her writing brought her enough money to buy a bigger house, she made her friends promise not to tell anyone her new address. It was difficult to suddenly be famous with your face in all the papers.

Newspaper **reviewers** have been full of praise for Joanne's books:

'The Harry Potter books are a series of stories adored by children and parents alike.'
        (Daily Telegraph, 1998)

'J.K. Rowling has woken up a whole generation to reading.'
        (The Times, 1998)

The life of a star

In 2000 Joanne travelled to the USA to promote *Harry Potter and the Prisoner of Azkaban*. She was amazed at the huge crowds in every city she visited. Arriving for a book-signing at a Boston bookshop, she saw a queue of people that went along the street and round the corner! Joanne says, 'I walked through the door and there was all this screaming and lots of flash bulbs going off. It was the nearest I'll ever come to being a pop star. I signed 1400 books that day.'

Harry's world

Readers say they love the way Joanne has created a whole world in Hogwarts, with its own history, magic, monsters and rules. You can 'live' in Harry Potter's world while you read a story. Then you can share in some of the Harry Potter magic in real life. You can play a Harry Potter computer game or make models of Hogwarts from special Lego kits. You can buy colouring books and wear a Harry Potter cape. You can even sleep under a Harry Potter duvet cover!

Books for charity

In 2001 the charity Comic Relief asked Joanne if she could help them raise money. She wrote two short books about the world of Hogwarts, *Quidditch Through the Ages* and *Fantastic Beasts and Where to Find Them,* and gave the money the books made to the charity. These books are both on the Hogwarts' reading list. Joanne used **pen names** for them, but of course no one but Joanne could have dreamt up all the 'facts' about Quidditch and magical animals.

▲ Joanne wrote several newspaper articles about the struggles she had bringing up her daughter on her own. She did this partly to support the National Council for One Parent Families, a charity that fights for the rights of single parents. Here she is supporting the charity.

J.K. Rowling on J.K. Rowling

Joanne is now the most famous children's writer in Britain, probably the world. Harry Potter fans are keen to know about the person behind the books and how she writes the stories they love to read. She has given many interviews. She also meets her readers and answers their questions. Here are some of her answers to questions she has been asked.

What Joanne says

Joanne has this advice for young people who want to write stories:

'Read as much as you can. Then start by writing about things you know – your own experiences, your own feelings. That's what I do.'

Do Hogwarts' students need to know things besides magic?
  'They can choose to study Muggle subjects. In the third book, Hermione takes the class Muggles Studies.'

If you could be a wizard, who would you be?
  'I'd probably be Hermione. She's a lot like me when I was younger. I wasn't that clever but I was definitely that annoying at times!'

How did you make the spells?
  'The spells are made up. I have met people who assure me that they are trying to do them, and I can assure them that they don't work.'

Friends are important in your books. What's the most important thing in friendship?
  'Acceptance and loyalty. There are enough people in the world to give you a hard time.'

How do you write long books without getting bored?
'I never get bored with the writing. I could (and often do) write all day and evening. I love being a writer.'

What will you do once you've finished the last Harry Potter book?
'It will be the most incredible thing to finish the books. It will have been a very long time to spend with those characters in my head. I'll be sad to leave them.'

What part of the whole Harry Potter success have you most enjoyed?
'Doing readings from my stories at bookshops and so on. It's the most fantastic experience: sitting in front of all these hundreds of people and hearing them laugh, answering their questions and hearing all they know about my characters.'

Will you always write?
'I'm sure I'll always write, at least until I lose my marbles. I'm a very, very lucky person, doing what I love best in all the world.'

▲ Children at a bookshop in New York, in 2000, start reading as they queue up to buy the latest Harry Potter book.

Films and the future

In 2000 Joanne's fourth book, *Harry Potter and the Goblet of Fire*, came out. Potter fans had been waiting longer this time and they got a much bigger book from Joanne. It became the fastest-selling book in history. Joanne made a special tour of Britain to **publicize** it. She travelled around on a steam train called the Hogwarts Express. The train left London from King's Cross Station, from a platform numbered $9\frac{3}{4}$ of course! A huge crowd of fans waved it off.

The Hogwarts Express arrives in Edinburgh with Joanne on board. This was just one of many stops on the way round Britain.

Harry in Hollywood

The same year a film of *Harry Potter and the Philosopher's Stone*, renamed *Harry Potter and the Sorcerer's Stone* in the USA, came out. Joanne was very involved in the making of the film.

The film was an enormous success. A film of the second book, *Harry Potter and the Chamber of Secrets*, came out in the autumn of 2002. Again there were queues of fans outside cinemas waiting to see their hero in the new adventure. Films are planned of all the other books, and will come out every year or year and a half.

The secret of success

Joanne has said she did not set out to write a certain sort of children's book – the idea for Harry Potter just 'fell into my head'. The books are exciting, scary and funny. There are things that are like normal life, and things that are pure, wonderful fantasy. Harry, Ron and Hermione are like ordinary children, except that they have magical adventures.

What Daniel Radcliffe says

Daniel Radcliffe was just eleven when he was chosen from thousands of boys to play Harry Potter in the film. He remembers the phone call:

'I was in the bath. Dad ran in and said "Guess who they want to play Harry Potter?" I started to cry. It was the best moment of my life.'

This picture of Daniel Radcliffe (Harry Potter), Emma Watson (Hermione Granger), and Rupert Grint (Ron Weasley) was taken after they were chosen for their roles in the first Harry Potter film.

Awards and more awards

Harry Potter and the Prisoner of Azkaban won the Whitbread Children's award in 1999 and in 2001 *Harry Potter and the Goblet of Fire* won the Children's Book Award in the 9–11 age range. Harry Potter books have won many other awards and prizes. Joanne was also awarded an **OBE** for services to children's literature. It was presented to her by Prince Charles at Buckingham Palace, London.

▲ The OBE Joanne received was awarded to her because of her work as a popular children's author. Here she is holding her medal at Buckingham Palace.

Joanne and Neil

In 2000 Joanne met Neil Murray, a doctor at an Edinburgh hospital. They enjoyed each other's company and started going out together. Joanne is a very famous person and some newspapers wrote stories about her new friendship. It is not easy having a private life when you are one of the most famous writers ever! Joanne is now a millionaire. She lives in a **mansion** in Edinburgh, and has another house in the middle of London with an underground swimming pool!

The work goes on!

Over 100 million copies of the Harry Potter books have been sold all over the world and they have been **published** in 55 different languages. After *Harry Potter and the Goblet of Fire* was published in 2000, Harry Potter fans had a three-year wait for the next book, *Harry Potter and the Order of the Phoenix*, which was 768 pages long. Joanne also found time to get married to Neil Murray in 2001 and their son, David, was born in March 2003.

Joanne still has more books to write to complete the series of adventures. Her plan is to make each new Harry Potter story longer, so that means much more writing. And there will be millions of eager fans waiting for each new book!

Find out more

The official J.K. Rowling fan club is the Bloomsbury Web Club at www.bloomsburymagazine.com/harrypotter/wizard/.

There are also many unofficial sites where you can read about Joanne and her books.

Timeline

1965 Joanne Rowling is born in Yate, near Bristol

1983 Goes to Exeter University in Devon, to study French

1990 Begins writing story that will become *Harry Potter and the Philosopher's Stone*

1991 Moves to Porto in Portugal to teach English

1993 Daughter Jessica is born in Porto. Moves to Edinburgh.

1994 Gets own flat in Leith on edge of Edinburgh. Lives on very little money.

1997–2003 Five *Harry Potter* titles are published

2001 Marries Dr Neil Murray

2003 Son David is born in Edinburgh

Books by J.K. Rowling

Here are the Harry Potter books written by Joanne so far:

Harry Potter and the Philosopher's Stone (Bloomsbury, 1997)
Harry Potter thinks he is just an ordinary boy, but finds out he is actually a wizard. Soon he is enrolled at Hogwarts School of Witchcraft and Wizardry.

Harry Potter and the Chamber of Secrets (Bloomsbury, 1998)
It is Harry's second year at Hogwarts and he has further magical adventures, and faces another battle with the forces of evil.

Harry Potter and the Prisoner of Azkaban (Bloomsbury, 1999)
There's a mass murderer on the loose and the mysterious prison guards of Azkabahan are guarding the school.

Harry Potter and the Goblet of Fire (Bloomsbury, 2000)
Hogwarts pupils compete in the Triwizard Tournament against two other famous schools of wizardry.

Harry Potter and the Order of the Phoenix (Bloomsbury, 2003)

Glossary

agent someone who helps writers with their careers, most importantly by finding publishers for their books

article piece of writing in a newspaper or magazine

comprehensive state school that provides the standard range of lessons, usually leading to GCSEs and A Levels

degree qualification that university students receive when they pass their final exams

divorce legal process, in which a marriage is officially ended

graduate to pass the final exams at university

Latin language that was spoken by the Romans. It used to be studied in most schools. Latin is often used for mottos and inscriptions on statues.

mansion very big, usually old, house

OBE (Order of the British Empire) medal awarded by the Queen to people who have done important things

pen name made-up name that authors sometimes use on their book

persecute treat people unfairly or cruelly

publicize make the public aware of something. For example, authors often do book signings at bookshops and give interviews.

publish when a publisher turns a story into a book that is sold in shops

publisher person or company that makes and sells books

posting place where people in the services (the army, navy and RAF) are sent to work

reviewer person who writes a review about a new film, book, music or art exhibition

social security (now called Jobseeker's Allowance) payment made by the government to people who do not have a job

Index

Titles in the *All About Authors* series are:

All about...

Malorie Blackman

Shaun McCarthy

Hardback   0 431 17982 4

All about...

Roald Dahl

Vic Parker

Hardback   0 431 17981 6

All about...

J.K. Rowling

Shaun McCarthy

Hardback   0 431 17980 8

All about...

Jacqueline Wilson

Vic Parker

Hardback   0 431 17983 2

Find out about the other titles in this series on our website www.heinemann.co.uk/library